OWLS

OWLS

OUR MOST CHARMING BIRD

MATT SEWELL

TEN SPEED PRESS
Berkeley

Copyright © 2014 by Matt Sewell

All rights reserved.
Published in the United States by Ten Speed Press,
an imprint of the Crown Publishing Group,
a division of Penguin Random House LLC, New York.
www.crownpublishing.com
www.tenspeed.com

Ten Speed Press and the Ten Speed Press colophon are
registered trademarks of Penguin Random House LLC.

Originally published in slightly different form
in Great Britain by Ebury Press, an imprint of Ebury Publishing,
a division of the Penguin Random House group, London, in 2014.

Library of Congress Cataloging-in-Publication Data

Sewell, Matt.
Owls : our most charming bird / Matt Sewell.—First American edition.
    pages cm
"Originally published in slightly different form…
by Ebury Press…, London, in 2014."
    1. Owls. I. Title.
    QL696.S8S49 2015
    598.9'7—dc23
                                2015013637
Hardcover ISBN: 978-1-60774-879-3
eBook ISBN: 978-1-60774-880-9

Printed in China

Series design by Two Associates; this edition compiled by Tash Webber

10 9 8 7 6 5 4 3 2 1

First American Edition

For my goldfinches, Jess, Romy, and Mae

CONTENTS

FOREWORD

Matt's charming book looks at our favorite nocturnal, nonchalant bird of prey: the owl. Wide-eyed in the still of night. Silent in flight. A strange rotating head. Imperious and haughty. It's not surprising the mysterious owl has meddled with people's minds. Through myth and folklore, we've managed to lay some peculiar extra baggage on these all-seeing, all-knowing creatures over the years. Holding vigils for virgins? Harbingers of horror? Wizards' wingmen? Or simply a marvellous niche invention for the afterhours?

Whatever they are up to, owls are a personal favorite of mine and my band, British Sea Power. On stage, we often employ decoy Long-Eared Owls, perching them on tree branches. They watch over us, staring out into the audience, giving us some added primeval stage presence. The owls are watching yoooouuu-ooooo.

Martin Noble

INTRODUCTION

It's simple: everybody loves owls! They are
all things for all men, women and children.
Owls are tough, wise, spooky, scary, majestic,
austere, spiritual, easy to draw, inspirational,
and cute.

In a work of wonder, every family of owl
has evolved totemic skills for survival
in habitats around the globe—the lush
woodlands of Europe, mountainside glades
of the Himalayas, savannahs of Africa, dust
bowls of the Americas, and the equatorial
tropical rainforests.

However we like to depict the owl—creepy
and haunting, or majestic and beautiful—their
singularity in the animal kingdom and their
unflinching colonization of our
Earth is simply breathtaking.

And that is why I love owls.

WOODLAND
OWLS

Barn Owl
Tyto alba

Easily one of the most beautiful, elegant
and enigmatic of all animals, never mind owls,
the Barn Owl is transcendent to view in
the wild: a shining pure illumination with
dark, unfathomably deep eyes.

They were not always viewed so kindly,
and so the legend of owls as cursed creatures,
ill-fated harbingers of destruction, was
born from this spectral bird, whose call is
a bloodcurdling shriek that could strip the
fingernails from all those unfortunate enough
to meet it. Superstitious folks would often nail
a wing—or even a whole Barn Owl—to a barn
door to keep out all witchery and evil doings,
so feared and ominous were these owls.

But however they got their name, Barn Owls
are a natural wonder. They are found all around
the world, moving with silent wingbeats, eyeing
you with a face you could never forget.

Eurasian Pygmy Owl
Glaucidium passerinum

This bushy-eyebrowed owl bumbles around
the woods hunting birds twice his size, like
a pocket-sized politician after a liquid lunch.
You can find variants of this little fellow in
woodlands across northern America, central
Europe and many parts of Asia. Depending
on where you're looking, you might spot the
Northern, Ferruginous, Andean, or Cuban
Pygmy Owl. But whichever one you see,
it will be roughly the height of a new
pencil—with much of that being its head.

Little Owl
Athene noctua

To us, the Little Owl is the small, dumpy one that sits on a fence post at dusk, watching the traffic fly by. But in days of yore, the mighty *Athene noctua* was a potent symbol of wisdom, good fortune, and sobriety. He was the bird of the Greek goddess Athena, upon whose shoulder he alighted—her sagacious terracotta-colored companion. This is the same Little Owl who is illustrated on ancient red pots in museums and iconized on charms and keepsakes in municipal markets and tourist traps across Greece.

The Acropolis was once full of Little Owls, living amongst the pillars and rocks, looking down upon a great civilization. Today, they are found across the whole of Europe and Asia.

Tawny Owl
Strix aluco

The Tawny Owl is perhaps the wisest of all our owls—or the wisest-looking anyway—and also a little bit forgetful, slapdash, sleepy, maybe even a little bit grumpy. As we know with all great brainiacs, their genius goes hand in hand with just as much of a lack of patience, self-hygiene, and common sense. Not that I'm saying that the Tawny is scruffy; it's just that he looks like he fell asleep and fell out of his tree into a big pile of leaves, and bumbled on with his day without sprucing himself back up again.

To be honest, owls aren't the brightest of birds, amazing as they are; parrots and crows are much smarter. It's all in the eyes: those magnificent piercing optics are what make all owls look like they are deep in concentrated scrutiny and steeped in long-lost knowledge.

Striped Owl
Pseudoscops clamator

The Striped Owl is the Long-Eared Owl's chilled-out cousin from South America...or is he? Scientists have struggled with the stripy genius's genus—so he has been awarded his own family name of *Pseudoscops*, along with a small handful of other rogue avian rarities. That's how he earned his stripes.

Aside from the sound-channeling facial disc, most of these owls have an amazing structural display of feathers across their chests—an arrangement as accomplished as Persian architecture; a perfect chaos governed by the mathematics of the universe.

Long-Eared Owl
Asio otus

A tall, elegant bird who would rather eat
you than do herself the disservice of actually
looking at you. With a scowl that could send
an icy shiver down the binoculars of whomever
dared to gaze upon her—before petrifying the
stoutest of hearts. Rendering you stricken like
a plastic bird scarer, an eternal statue, with
internal nightmares of past fashion choices…
"Did I really wear that anorak?" Moody.

Short-Eared Owl
Asio flammeus

Caught in the sunny daytime after she has been
up all night, with a face like thunder, mid-walk
of shame, flying over open ground looking for
her purse, mascara smeared, with a beast of a
hangover. Don't get in her way, don't talk to
her, just let her do what she's doing so she can
get back to bed. She needs her shut-eye.

Jamaican Owl
Pseudoscops grammicus

As the name suggests, this rufous owl
is found only on that beautiful island in
the West Indies. Another anomaly for the
scientists, what with their Eagle-Owl ears
and the semblance of a stupendous "scops"
owl—and so we have another curious entrant
in the exclusive *Pseudoscops* subdivision.

Sadly, our friend is not a great traveler and not
a fraction as successful as many of Jamaica's
other exports that have circumnavigated the
globe. If only they were as popular as reggae,
they wouldn't be on the endangered list.

Collared Scops Owl
Otus lettia

A witch's tapestry of dusty moth's wing,
flaked pages from an alchemist's compendium,
lichen, and moss, intricately woven together
with spiders' webs and swallow's spit. This
enormous-eyed sprite is found high in the
trees of temperate forests across much of
Asia. It's easy to see why a bird as bizarre and
curious-looking as the Collared Scops has been
associated with magical myths and properties
from all corners of the Far East.

Northern Saw-Whet Owl
Aegolius acadicus

OMG SO CUUUTE!!!
Yup, the Northern Saw-Whet Owl is an
absolute darling, with a permanent look
of surprise spread across its adorable little
face. Smaller-than-a-blackbird and
fluffier-than-a-three-week-old-Labrador,
it's pleading puppy-dog eyes
look at you like you're about to give
him the biggest chocolate mouse he has
ever seen. It's one of the smallest owls in
North America, and just as popular with
bird lovers as it is with ALL CAP
shouters on YouTube.

Barred Owl
Strix varia

An owl walks into a bar.

The bartender says, "I'm not serving you!"

The owl asks, "Why not?"

"Because you're barred!"

(Sorry.)

Bar jokes aside, the Barred Owl is a large, rather stocky owl, a beautiful resident of mature forests in northwestern and eastern North America. Though quite common, he retains a mystique, looking like a nomad of the forest with exotic gypsy blood, shrouded in a headscarf, asking his classic question:

"Who cooks for you? Who cooks for you-all?"

Certainly not the bartender!

TROPICAL
OWLS

Greater Sooty Owl
Tyto tenebricosa

A negative Barn Owl. Many Australian animals
are a bit dark, from the bloodthirsty crocs
to the highly poisonous spiders and snakes.
There is even a massive emu relative called a
Cassowary that can rear up and disembowel
any foolish backpacker getting in its way.

But this goth Barn Owl is not dangerous
in any way—except to the small rodents and
bugs that he stalks through the eucalyptus
forests of northern Australia, his jet-black
wizard's cloak contrasting brilliantly with his
white markings, shining as bright as the stars
of the southern hemisphere.

Oriental Bay Owl
Phodilus badius

If people in the olden days thought Barn Owls were spooky and cursed, just imagine what they would have made of an Oriental Bay Owl. A twisted vision, a nightmare stalker, a vile monstrosity!

Owls have been used symbolically in art for centuries; their looming presence, bloodcurdling calls, and fearsome hunting techniques have represented nightmares and oft evoked a sense of foreboding and horror. So although this is practically a *Tyto* family member, I still can't help but picture it as the wretched soul of a beloved Barn Owl trapped in purgatory. And that is exactly why they still have a power over the human race—the owls are not what they seem…

Maned Owl
Jubula lettii

Deep in the rainforests of Western Africa,
a maned hunter basks in his kingdom, but
this one has tufts and tassels rather than
a thick imperial beard, and he probably
has one mate—if he's lucky—rather than a
harem at the command of his padded talons.
But still, he is an amazing-looking owl,
whomever you want to compare him to.

Spectacled Owl
Pulsatrix perspicillata

Dwelling in the lush rainforests of
Central America, striking, handsome and
uncomplicated, the Spectacled Owls have
no need for camouflage. Just a distinguishing
pair of eyeglasses to cut them a fly look
in the jungle.

But watch out: their wide-eyed optimistic
beam can quickly switch to a malevolent glare.
Much as an exasperated teacher might fix you
with an icy stare above her bifocals. Chilling.

Long-Whiskered Owlet
Xenoglaux loweryi

Who have we got here, then? Despite an appearance to the contrary, this is a fully grown Pygmy Owl and not a baby career-politician—a wild-eyebrowed, know-it-all toddler perched on a leather chesterfield giving his opinionated opinions to the rest of the woods.

So don't let his overabundant whiskers and bookish demeanor put you off: the Long-Whiskered Owlet is an amazing bird, found solely in the cloud forests on the hills of the Andes in Peru—a magical, impenetrable land that has gone untouched by civilization for millennia and is home to so many other natural wonders as yet unknown to humankind. Let's just try to let them be.

Black-and-White Owl
Strix nigrolineata

This pied owl is a desperado of the subtropical forests of Central America, a smart stippled bird donning a bandito mask to rob the hot, damp woodland of its cicadas.

Although they do see very well in the dark, all owls have very bad eyesight close up—and won't be able to tell if you're sticking your tongue out at them. Handy. Yet all possess a moustache of stiff whiskery feathers around the beak, which are an essential tool for hunting any time of the day.

Spotted Wood Owl
Strix seloputo

One of the round-headed earless *Strix* owls,
the Spotted Wood-Owl is found in widely
scattered areas of Southeast Asia. Though
gorgeous, he is more often heard by night
than seen by day. His mellow single hoots,
cutting through the trill and chatter of other
jungle nightlife, sound like the subdued *woofs*
of a dog who's trying very, very hard not to
wake you. Or you may hear his deep, rising,
persistent chuckle: whatever the joke,
he finds it hilarious!

Buff-Fronted Owl
Aegolius harrisii

What a dull name for such a visually vibrant
owl! It's a shame the experts who named him
concentrated on the buff chest rather than
the massive "V" emblazoned across his face.
How could you miss that?

With this chap, "V" most definitely stands for
"verve"; and also for "Venezuela," which is one
of the countries in Central America where you
will find him, as well as many other species
of our amazing tropical owls.

Fearful Owl
Nesasio solomonensis

What an awesome name for a beast of an owl, with his razor-sharp claws, bulky frame and vexed facial markings. The "X" across his countenance illuminates a terrifying beak that strikes fear into any possum, phalanger, parrot, or poacher that treads through the forests of the Fearful Owl.

Not much is known about this fellow, being a rare breed living in inhospitable terrain. He does look very similar to the bygone Laughing Owl from New Zealand, which is sadly extinct. With deforestation and decreasing food sources in the Solomon Islands, this could very easily be the fate of this rare owl too.

Maybe that's why he is so fearful.

Crested Owl
Lophostrix cristata

Another owl from the Neotropics and found
all across Central and South America. Roughly
the size of a Barn Owl—but those eyebrows
must measure him up against an Eagle-Owl.
What incredible appendages! They are very
handy, and not just to fan our hero in the
hot, humid jungle. In fact, they are used in
a variety of ways. Straight up or tucked away
when he's feeling threatened and pretending
to be a branch; out at 45 degrees when he is
alert; flopped out and hanging down
sideways when he's just chillin', man.

Brown Fish Owl
Bubo zeylonensis

A large eagle-owl like this chap was probably once a barbarian meat-lover who found himself trapped in a spot with just seafood for dinner, took a liking to it, and then turned pescatarian. So, through time and evolution, he has done away with the facial disc of a sound-hunting owl to develop a sharper, eagle-like head. Who needs ears to catch a fish, anyway? When was the last time you heard a trout?

The Brown Fish Owl was always believed to be a bird of Asia and the Middle East—until some keen-eyed birder discovered a pair flying across a beautiful lake idyll hidden away in Turkey. The owls settled in and have fledged into a nice colony of Baykus—which translates to Mr. Bird. Finally: a little bit of respect!

African Wood Owl
Strix woodfordii

He's from Africa, and he lives in the woods.

A recognizable relative of our Tawny Owl, his coat echoes his surroundings just as much as the tangerine-and-chestnut outfit of the fine Tawny mirrors the lush copse that he calls home. With the jungle's dense bronze-and-auburn tones highlighted with white spots—which look like stars reflected in the still, sepia pools of the rainforest—the African Wood Owl wears his heart on his sleeve.

WILDERNESS
OWLS

Ural Owl
Strix uralensis

Am I allowed to have a favorite? If I were,
it would certainly be the lovely Ural Owl.
They haunt the Ural mountain forests and
Siberian steppes like friendly ghosts, with their
coats the color of smoke flecked with ash,
their immense midnight eyes that you could
drown in, and a big tough beak that clacks like
coconut husks. Their presence is pleasant and
can seem somewhat dainty, but as with
all owls, appearances can be deceptive. The
Ural Owl is known as one of the toughest
owls around—and rules his patch as
mercilessly as a Mongol Khan.

Scops Owl
Otus scops

There are little Scops Owls pretending
to be branches, keeping themselves tucked
away in every corner of the world where it is
warm. This common Scops is Europe's entry
in what is probably the biggest genus of owl
species. They come in a range of different
shapes, sizes, and color tones, but all have
charming, tufty ears and an amazing flecked
pattern: a dazzling camouflage for
the dense woodland, tropical rainforest,
and bamboo thickets in which they
hide and reside.

Flammulated Owl
Psiloscops flammeolus

I was a bit disappointed when I looked up "flammulated" in the dictionary; it doesn't mean "flammable feathers," nor is it a fancy phrase for a forest fire. It just means "a reddish color," which, if you ask me, is a bit of a dull moniker for one of the oddest and smallest owls in America—especially when you factor in a coat of feathers as incredible as hers. She looks like a little wet owl who has been rolled in a dusty elixir—a potion concocted from a pinch of leaves from an autumnal, amber forest floor, which are then delicately crushed to a fiery dust and transfused with a handful of sparks, and a bit of eye of newt and toe of frog mixed in for good measure. Magic!

Eurasian Eagle-Owl
Bubo bubo

With talons like a butcher's hooks, wings like saloon doors, a massive neck like a Turkish weightlifter's—this owl has a swagger like he knows everybody in the room—and knows everybody is scared of him. Yet he's still approachable and actually very likeable.

If you ever visit an owl center in Europe or the UK, you may get to hold one. This enormous, elephantine owl is happy to stand on your begloved, beloved hand—but just as you are starting to feel comfortable, it may well give you a look as if to say: "Oi, I'm in charge and I can easily snap that hand clean off." Gulp!

Blakiston's Fish Owl
Bubo blakistoni

Whose style is less elegant fly fisherman and more like a poacher on a moonless night? Who waits in the shadows, perched on bankside stumps, coarse trousers held up with a length of bailing twine, ferret in his back pocket and a brace of pheasants over his shoulder? There, on low-slung branches, he lingers, waiting to drop down into the icy waters to grope for unsuspecting fish in the chilling mountain streams of Japan and Russia.

Snowy Owl
Bubo scandiacus

———————————

A coat of the purest white and an icy stare
as piercing as an arctic breeze. Females and
the young have coal-black spots and bars,
but all are magnificently milky: a perfect
camouflage, much better than that of polar
bears and arctic foxes, who of course are white,
but have a wee bit of a yellowy tint against
their bleached surroundings.

A monarch of the tundra, the Snowy Owl is
a whopper, close to an eagle-owl in height
and hunting prowess, feeding upon lemmings,
ptarmigans, and other winter fare by snatching
her prey with her massive moonboots. To
protect against the cruel temperatures of the
arctic, her feet are ensconced in thick feathers,
styled in a brilliance of frosted white.

Hawk Owl
Surnia ulula

Here we have a precise and vicious
pursuer of voles and other small fluffy
rodents, chasing them through the cold,
pine-scented forests of the northern part
of America, Canada, Scandinavia,
Russia, and China.

The Huntsman: he has the eyes of a hawk,
the long tail of a hawk, the low mean brow
of a hawk, and the stripy T-shirt of a hawk—
whilst also possessing the bulky wings of
an owl, the specialized facial disk of an owl,
and the feather-taloned boots of an owl.
When you combine these special weapons
and tactics, you can have nothing but
the unique…Hawk Owl!

Great Gray Owl
Strix nebulosa

Yes, he is great, isn't he? With a head like a
geodesic dome inhabited by a bunch of strung-
out hippies, the Great Gray Owl looks like
he's been hanging out with these guys for some
time. With a wide-eyed mellowness, he takes
in the world at his own pace.

But don't let that mellow vibe fool you: hidden
within that massive owl-down jacket is a
stealthy hunter whose body was built to survive
the glacial northern quarters of the world in
Asia, America, and Europe. His tightly knitted
helmet works as an intricate feathered vortex,
channelling the sound of mice going about
their day under thick snow. The Great Gray
Owl tunes into the vibrations emanating from
the rodents' networked tunnels...and expertly
drops down to pick out his prey. An energy-
saving tactic to survive the bitter conditions
of his subzero domain.

Boreal Owl
Aegolius funereus

Another owl from the same dense hyperborean forests as the Hawk Owl, found around the world just before the trees meet the tundra. An owl with many a moniker, it is known more commonly in Europe as Tengmalm's Owl, but it also answers to Richardson's Owl and Pearly Owl. But I like "Boreal," as it is basically a fancy way of saying "cold forest."

Whatever you want to call it, you can always recognize it as the owl with the head the shape of an upside-down dumpster—or, to give it a scientific twist—a Boreal Owl with a crown like a wobbly trapezium.

Giant Scops Owl
Otus gurneyi

In the kingdom of the minuscule Scops, you don't have to be much bigger than a pigeon to be regarded as colossal amongst your equals. This tiny giant strides across his teeny kingdom—made up of only three small mountainous islands in the Philippines—with plumage as strikingly cheerful and sanguine as an equinoctical sun. Positive is what he needs to be, as deforestation and mining are flattening his home and destroying his habitat.

Jungle Owlet
Glaucidium radiatum

This owl could easily sit on your shelf:
a polished teak talisman, a memento of your
travels to distant misty lands. Not much
bigger than a bullfinch, this toy-sized owl has
a beautiful plot that he can call home. His
stomping ground is the moist deciduous forest
that stretches all the way across the foothills
of the Himalayas. What a view!

He may be small, but he certainly knows how
to pick the best neck of the woods.

DESERT
OWLS

Northern White-Faced Owl
Ptilopsis leucotis

With the waxy whiskers of a Mandarin
kung-fu wizard, the Northern White-Faced
Owl from the savannahs of Africa is
a magnificent magician of mutation.

At ease, the Northern White-Faced Owl
is quite handsome and striking, with his
monochrome face, orange eyes, and silver-
fox moustache. Under threat from a similar-
sized villain, he fans his wings and bobs his
head with fantastical fiery eyes—an awesome
defensive tactic used by many owls. But in the
presence of a larger predator, he draws in all
his feathers, turns sideways, and makes himself
as slim as possible. With squinting eyes and a
beak completely covered in an oily brush, the
owl now resembles a braided branch. Not the
least bit handsome—and essentially invisible.

Great Horned Owl
Bubo virginianus

From his leafy temple in the North
Country to the desert wastelands of the
Deep South, the Worshipful Master of
the Americas governs the land with iron
talons. An aggressive predator who demands
respect, he appears like the ancient god
Moloch, presiding over somber sacrificial
rites in the torch-lit caves of his ancestors.
Easily the largest owl of the land,
and effortlessly the most dangerous:
the all-seeing head of the totem pole.

Southern Boobook Owl
Ninox novaeseelandiae

Bubuk is the Aboriginal name for this
small hawk owl; it's a term used widely across
Australia to describe a variety of owls. Its
other names include Ngugug, Morepork,
and Mopoke, which are all onomatopoeias
describing the gruff croak of Australia's
smallest and most common owl.

All owls have fourteen vertebrae in
their long necks—that's twice as many as
us humans—and they can turn their heads
almost completely upside down. 'Struth!

Spotted Eagle-Owl
Bubo africanus

Yes, it's got ear tufts, making it an
Eagle-Owl, and spots, making it a Spotted
Eagle-Owl. But that's rather prosaic-sounding
for a wonderfully illuminated bird like this,
which looks as though it's made out of
delicate, crisp layers of Viennetta ice cream
and 90-percent dark chocolate drops.

At eighteen inches tall, this gent is one of the
smaller owls, but quite a common and most
welcome sighting with the binoculars if you
are out birding in the hot, arid woodland of
northern Africa or the Arabian Peninsula.

For a bird with ice-cream feathers, only
one label will suffice: cool owl!

Verreaux's Eagle-Owl
Bubo lacteus

All right, cheeky! Who are you batting
those lashes at?

As owls go, the Verreaux's is up there with
the biggest and heaviest—but that only
means he weighs the same as a hedgehog.
It's those hollow bones and the hunter
diet that keeps him trim.

This African eagle-owl of the Sahara is
a perfect example of how owls' specialist
eyesight works. Those heavy lids protect
the binocular-like, tubular eyes that sit still
and stationary inside the sockets—unlike
our eyeballs, which can roll around. To
compensate for the lack of movement, they
bob their heads to and fro and twist their
necks around 270 degrees. That's not all the
way around; if they tried that,
their heads would pop off!

Pel's Fishing Owl
Scotopelia peli

The African fishing owls are a different
kettle of fish from the Asian fishing owls.
They are much more proud of their
appearance and don't have the funny
shrunken-head thing going on.

Pel's is quite the opposite, in fact,
and is able to flare her fine head of feathers
into a glorious rufous full crown when the
mood takes her. It must be one of the finest
sights in nature to see a Pel's Fishing Owl
in its natural surroundings.

Elf Owl
Micrathene whitneyi

As you can imagine, the Elf Owl is one of our smallest owls. A member of the Pygmy family, it inhabits the famous Wild West deserts of the USA and Mexico.

I think it would be fair to say that the Elf Owl loves cacti, especially the saguaro—the iconic type that stands sentinel and looks like a silhouette of a swollen, surrendering cowboy (without a hat) against the red desert sky.

It's no wonder the Elf Owl loves them—the cacti are an ecosystem that provides everything our friend needs. Food: the insects visiting the cactus's flowers and fruit. Shade: from the searing desert sun. Shelter: our owl nests in cavities carved out by sap-loving woodpeckers. What's not to love?

Powerful Owl
Ninox strenua

I doff my cap to the pioneer in deepest
Australia who first clapped eyes on this
strapping beast—probably while it was
ripping off a koala's head—and baptized
it the Powerful Owl.

Bounding in at over two feet high,
it's a member of the hawk family, so it has
a strange, round head like a hairy buzzard's,
with a cleaver-like beak and feet like
sharpened anchors.

As you can tell from its great name, the
Powerful is the largest and most feared
Australian owl.

Burrowing Owl
Athene cunicularia

This stern little troglodyte, a member
of the Little Owl family, has found
himself a unique roosting style amongst his
peers. A bird of the Americas, living wherever
there are dry ranges and open grassland—or,
to be precise, the panoramas where you will
find prairie dogs and their burrows, as that
is where the Burrowing Owl likes to make
his home.

You can't see his legs in this illustration,
as he is obviously burrowing, but they are
actually quite long, and he is a remarkable
sprinter—just as agile on the foot as on the
wing, and a hunter with prodigious talents.
The Burrowing Owl even inspired the
Native Americans to herald him as a
protective spirit for their warriors.

Stygian Owl
Asio stygius

An even moodier Long-Eared Owl—how can this be? I had heard talk of such a phantom, and my eyes do not deceive me! The Stygian Owl is a shadowy, horned apparition that haunts Central and South America, with a death-like glare—and a name to match.

"Stygian" is derived from the River Styx, the waterway of Greek myth. There is a saying, "as dark as the River Styx," and it was a murky place indeed: a grim course of black water, where the Reaper-like boatman Charon ferried the souls of the dead to the underworld kingdom of Hades. It seems like the ancient Greeks felt the same way about Long-eared Owls as I do, but to be honest, I am more concerned about the demonic Great Horned Owl than the grumpy Stygian and his cantankerous *Asio* brothers.

Brown Wood Owl
Strix leptogrammica

An owl made of mahogany, with a facial-disc
fade of titian red to fresh ginger—so not just
"brown," and therefore deserving of a much
better name. Even the mouthful of her species
name of *leptogrammica* just means "finely
barred," which she most certainly is. However,
on inspection, the plumage of all large owls
is a striking lattice of layered softness: the
feathers have a velvet comb of serrated tips that
cushion sound and aid the flight of
these hushed silent hunters.

Dusky Eagle-Owl
Bubo coromandus

A ravishing khaki owl of India and
Southeast Asia. The life of a Dusky sounds
like nirvana—his bungalow is built in the
cool, leafy heights of an old mango or tamarind
tree, with its veranda facing the riverside.
Here, escaping the hullabaloo, he and his good
wife reside all year round and take tiffin at
dusk, consisting of the local avifauna.
Sounds pukka.

Omani Owl
Strix omanensis

Last but by no means least, here we have
an owl who was very late to the party—so late,
in fact, that if I had created this book just a
year earlier, this fine bird would not have
even been discovered yet.

The rocky, scattered hillside groves of Oman
in the Middle East are where two expert
bird-sound recordists chanced upon this rare
Arabian treasure. Very much a desert owl in
coloring—but with long legs, orange eyes,
and a distinct call to set it apart from the
Hulme's Tawny Owl of the same locality.
All of these characteristics immediately
alerted the recordists that they had discovered
a new species to add to our wonderful world
of owls. Let's raise a glass to the guys with
the sound approach.

SPOTTING AND JOTTING

It's great to spot an owl you've never seen before, so to keep track here's a handy way to jot it down. Get spotting by either sitting comfortably at your window, or packing your boots, a flask and binoculars, and going on your travels across the globe. Happy spotting!

☐ Barn Owl

☐ Eurasian Pygmy Owl

 ☐ Little Owl

 ☐ Tawny Owl

 ☐ Striped Owl

☐ Long-Eared Owl

☐ Short-Eared Owl

☐ Jamaican Owl

☐ Collared Scops Owl

☐ Northern Saw-Whet Owl

☐ Barred Owl

☐ Greater Sooty Owl

☐ Oriental Bay Owl

☐ Maned Owl

☐ Spectacled Owl

☐ Long-Whiskered Owlet

☐ Black-and-White Owl

☐ Spotted Wood Owl

☐ Buff-Fronted Owl

☐ Fearful Owl

☐ Crested Owl

☐ Brown Fish Owl

☐ African Wood Owl

☐ Ural Owl

☐ Scops Owl

☐ Flammulated Owl

☐ Eurasian Eagle-Owl

☐ Blakiston's Fish Owl

☐ Snowy Owl

☐ Hawk Owl

☐ Great Gray Owl

☐ Boreal Owl

☐ Giant Scops Owl

☐ Jungle Owlet

☐ Northern White-Faced Owl

☐ Great Horned Owl

☐ Southern Boobook Owl

☐ Spotted Eagle-Owl

☐ Verraux's Eagle-Owl

☐ Pel's Fishing Owl

☐ Elf Owl

☐ Powerful Owl

☐ Burrowing Owl

 ☐ Stygian Owl

 ☐ Brown Wood Owl

 ☐ Dusky Eagle-Owl

 ☐ Omani Owl

ACKNOWLEDGMENTS

Thank you to:

The Goldfinches, the Sewells, the Roses,
and the Lees.

Martin Noble, Simon Benham, Nicki, Jeff,
Robin, and Andrew at Caught By The River.

Fizz, Jambo, Milley, Pip, Boo, Paul, and
Mark at Battlefield Falconry Centre.

Phil Aylen, Edward Lear, Eleazar Albin,
Boran Biriz, Roy Wilkinson, Ceri Levi,
and the Internet.

Find out more about Matt and his work at
www.mattsewell.co.uk

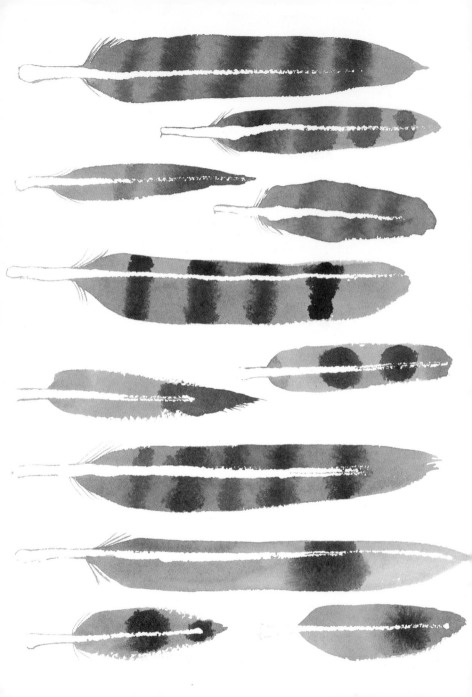